RED

Linda France

RED

BLOODAXE BOOKS

ISBN: 1 85224 178 0

First published 1992 by
Bloodaxe Books Ltd,
P.O. Box 1SN,
Newcastle upon Tyne NE99 1SN.

Bloodaxe Books Ltd acknowledges
the financial assistance of Northern Arts.

For Simon

Cover reproduction by V & H Reprographics, Newcastle upon Tyne.

Cover printing by J. Thomson Colour Printers Ltd, Glasgow.

Printed in Great Britain by
Bell & Bain Limited, Glasgow, Scotland.

*I'm not coming to the revolution
unless there's dancing.*

EMMA GOLDMAN

Acknowledgements

Acknowledgements are due to the editors of the following publications in which some of these poems first appeared: *Evening Chronicle* (Newcastle), *Foolscap, Frogmore Papers, Hard Times* (Berlin), *Iron, London Magazine, Manchester Poetry 3, New Prospects, The North, Poetry Durham, The Rialto, South-West Poetry Competition Anthology, Scratch, Stand, The Wide Skirt,* and *Writing Women.*

Several of these poems appeared in Carol Rumens' anthology *New Women Poets* (Bloodaxe Books, 1990), and 'Susan Martin, Painter's Wife' was featured in *Fire and Brimstone*, a poetry and music collaboration premièred at the 1989 Hexham Abbey Festival. 'Acts of Love' won the Basil Bunting Award in the Newcastle *Evening Chronicle* Poetry Competition in 1988, and 'If Love Was Jazz' won the same prize again in the 1989 competition. *Acts of Love* was published as a pamphlet by the Echo Room Press in 1989.

'On the Circle Line' and 'Imaginary Landscape with Real Horse' were read on *Wordworks* (Tyne Tees Television) and published in the Wordworks anthology (Bloodaxe Books/Tyne Tees Television, 1992). 'If Love Was Jazz' was read on *Celebration* (Tyne Tees Television, 1990). 'North and South' and 'If Love Was Jazz' were broadcast on *Third Opinion* (BBC Radio 3), and 'Runaway' was read on Wear FM (Sunderland).

I would like to thank Northern Arts for a Writer's Award given in 1989 and for a Tyrone Guthrie Award in 1990. I am also grateful to Bernard and Mary Loughlin at Annaghmakerrig.

Contents

Hennaing My Hair

A man I know brought me henna
from the Souk in Marrakech.
The old Moroccan apothecary creased his eyes,
offered a love potion of crushed insects.
My friend only took the henna, so he says,
a plump parcel of foreign khaki powder.

It seems as if Mrs Grieve doesn't approve
of such unashamed exotica –
only the shortest of entries in her *Modern Herbal* –
'Other names: Mehndi, Al-Khanna,
Jamaica Mignonette' – a harem herb,
for female adornment, pleasure.

I mix the henna, with hot water,
to a thick spinachy mud,
spread it on my head, recklessly.
Wet brown clods splatter sink, floor,
me. The whole morning I'm turbaned,
irresistibly aware of my hair, alchemy.

After four heady hours, I rinse it off,
the provocative sculpture my hair's become.
It takes more water than they see a month
in Marrakech to wash it clean,
to shampoo out the last grainy residue.
The suds foam ochre.

I towel hair I think's returned to normal
but, as it dries, my forehead's wisped
with curling copper filaments;
my head's on fire, brazenly aflame,
a red as wild, as cunning
as a vixen on heat.

Better, I think, than aphrodisiacs.

Bed and Breakfast in the City of Culture

Not-quite-spring-meadow curtains didn't meet,
fenced by a grey mesh of netted window,
receding out-of-focus tenement systems.
Quilt and sheets, wallpaper, carpet and chair –
seed-packet hybrid reds and pinks – shrieked
as shrill as the door-bell at 1 a.m:
a malt-mouthed Yorkshire drawl, *fucking* everything
fucking. We already had. Now forged into spoons
for morning tongues – salt, porridge, mint.

Things we didn't photograph but print
their images in my mind just as the way
our familiar bodies whispered a foreign language
in the dark dashed by the lobby light
beneath the door: our esperanto
of lips and skin; suitcase, a bulky chaperone;
toothbrushes' tartan green and red coupling
on the sink, filmed with layers of other visitors' dirt;
one whose name in the register we shared, *France, Harrogate.*

Nothing good comes from too much thinking
our landlady told us, arms full of eggs,
in an East European accent more tempting
than the polyglot toast, marmalade
encapsulated in plastic. Derek from Oxford
reeled off numbers of motorways – M8, 74 –
like so many conquests. Under the table
I wrapped my second egg like a warm pink baby
in a paper napkin, stowed it in my pocket.

Breadwinner

Midway between sponge and knead,
your strong sweet back seizes;
and you're a bent French stick.
Fretful, I soothe you between sheets,
pour brandy. Later, returning to the bowl
brimming with creamy yeast, no expert,
I mix in flour, salt, already weighed.
The stiff dough fails to yield to my tender touch.
It's all lumps, I lean on, like dust, clay:

where are you now when I need you most?

This is man's work, building bricks
of dough to rise and change with time
and heat into bread. I soldier on.
By the third loaf, I'm making less
of a sow's ear, fewer San Andreas faults.
But it still looks nothing like *Sunblest,
Mother's Pride*. I'm a wife who wants
a wife. And it's only when you're flat
on your back, I know that's what I've got:

your way with bread; your slow, firm rise.

Bus Driver

He has some crack for everyone,
has Joe – transporting his cargo
across the high seas of the shire.
All of *us* are female,
but *he's* at the helm, our figurehead.

His blue and white bus is all red
inside. The effect abattoir, or womb –
appropriate for transition, from A to B.
For Joe, it's A to bloody B
and back again four times daily.
He gave up smoking, couldn't stick it.

My funny hat confuses him. He's curious.
Over the jutting backs of seats, we chat.
'Where's the money in poems?'
he replies, when I confess I write.
'A Jackie Collins. That's what they want.
Fantasy. Romance.' Joe knows.

By, he could tell some tales –
the busfulls of women
who don't get enough. Joe fancies
a poem for him, and his bus.
This is it. No frills.

On the Circle Line

If Freud was right concerning trains in dreams,
Why is mine always in the wrong station?
If, in bed, all is not what it seems,
Why's it so hard to resist temptation?

It's easy to guess the derivation
Of his hypothesis, his phallic themes;
But it's still open to arbitration
If Freud was right concerning trains in dreams.

But I wake myself up with primal screams
When I find I've got no reservation.
When I can see how the iron horse steams,
Why is mine always in the wrong station?

An excellent means of transportation,
Even though it may take you to extremes;
But is it worth all the aggravation
If, in bed, all is not what it seems?

I'm not the sort of person who esteems
A snail's trail – life without titivation.
Right this minute I could write reams and reams
Why it's so hard to resist temptation.

Whatever the nocturnal assignation,
Between the sheets, or in my day-time dreams,
I can't ignore the implication
Of the tannoy voice announcing it seems
That Freud was right...

Precious Stones

The gold was old even then – smooth, yellow
and beautiful – a small treasure glinting
in the gimcrack arcade junk shop window.
And it was ours – after months of skimping.
Six bright stones crowned the bevelled band – ruby,
emerald, garnet, amethyst, ruby,
diamond – an Edwardian whimsy
spelling *Regard*. I wore it facing me.
Now I wear the years in between – fine lines
etching my eyes, hair traced with grey – rarely
the ring on my third finger; emptiness
where the garnet and amethyst should be.
Every year at Christmas we exchange cards –
I hesitate before writing *Regards*.

Digging Potatoes

Enter said the blush of wine,
Rosehip candlelight.
Continue said my eyes,
As you made love to me
From the other side of the room.

In the darkness of the car
You dazzled me, like headlights,
And made me shiver,
As if I needed some choke.

What could I do but give you
Potatoes and no promises;
And tell you now that the flower
Down from the mill, by the river's edge,
You thought might be agrimony –
Its name is yellow loosestrife.

That's what I wish for you:
No troubles;
Only the sound of water
Nearby, and potatoes.

Dreaming True

I

Her father's voice lit up the corners of the house,
old show tunes from *South Pacific, Carousel.*

'If you don't have a dream,
how you gonna have a dream come true?'

Her mother tells her she thinks too much.
'It'll only end in tears.'

Their daughter counts sheep's eye stars,
tumbles into a lumpy fleece of sleep.

The tape loops – *playback, fast forward.*
No *stop, eject*; her tears.

II

For years she's dreamed
of holding science like a globe in her hand,
of slipping on space like a leather glove,
of a singular woman, naked as an eye, far-sighted, herself.

Now she tilts her head, sees a shower of stars,
trailing prongs of paradox, perfection.
They light up her palm and she follows the lines,
sees where they cross.

And it's all hers –
every single star, every shred of darkness,
all she needs to be,
fears, dreams.

III

The telephone trembles in the silent room.
A policeman tells a woman,
in a lazy voice, her son's alone
in a strange house. His father's gone.

The child stabbed his panic into 999.
The woman grips the hard plastic.
She's a hundred miles away;
while her son tries to make policemen understand –

animals skating on a white fridge;
sheep chewing grass, dirty glass;
jars of beans, in rows, staring;
curtains like red doors, doors like green curtains.

Five days before, she dreamt it:
a maze of terraced houses, smoky brick;
a child running from door to door,
trying to find his way home.

And her, somewhere else,
dressed in menace.
It tumbled her awake.
She had to write it down.

'Dreaming true' they call it;
in tune with inevitability.
She'd rather sing another melody
where dreams know their place –

fat pillows, warm beds –
not out on the streets,
                        running.

IV

Believing dreams come true,
truth's just a nightmare, is perhaps
(hurricanes, earthquakes, aircrashes, bombs)
madness.

An attempt to make sense
of bright dreams and black stars:
not to pretend
you can keep it all neat,

separate.
All's one and all's not;
truth plays tricks and dreams flame
epiphanies. Both pin you

to the centre of where you are,
transformed by space,
naked,
singular.

Herpes

Something has put its foot
in my mouth, stamped its spoor

on my lips. If I laugh I'll crack
like packed arid earth. Wordless,

all mouth, I'm a lamprey
swallowing shoals of blank verse.

Yesterday's flames have left me
scorched. Even air burns

me. My tender, my sacred place
defiled, I am zoneless.

This is where scab moths build their nests,
this pulsing tumulus;

no one cares what's buried there:
a Pandora's box of curses,

lid trellissed with scarlet
hearts, masquerade blessings,

worms. My mouth aches with so much
nothing, starved of kisses,

infected with the grit
of shipwrecked pearls.

A Woman Called Faithless

There's a woman called Faithless
living in my house.

She moves from room to room,
trailing musk and ambergris.

Mouth parted, faintly bruised,
she is moody as seaweed. Her glad

gull's eye collects shells, bones.
Her favourite haunt is horizontal.

A creature wearing only a necklace
of names, she is all things to all men.

You can count on her to kiss and tell.
I think she's a swan on holiday:

fascinating from across a lake;
all beak and hissing when you get close.

I watch her giving the Man of the House
the largest slice of cake. I know her

too well; I cannot trust her.
She's Faithless, as a cat;

steals love from cupboards.

If Love Was Jazz

If love was jazz,
I'd be dazzled
By its razzmatazz.

If love was a sax
I'd melt in its brassy flame
Like wax.

If love was a guitar,
I'd pluck its six strings,
Eight to the bar.

If love was a trombone,
I'd feel its slow
Slide, right down my backbone.

If love was a drum,
I'd be caught in its snare,
Kept under its thumb.

If love was a trumpet,
I'd blow it.

If love was jazz,
I'd sing its praises,
Like Larkin has.

But love isn't jazz.
It's an organ recital.
Eminently worthy,
Not nearly as vital.

If love was jazz,
I'd always want more.
I'd be a regular
On that smoky dance-floor.

Acts of Love

The question is: why, if my utopia doesn't
contain men, are you my utopia?

ANN OAKLEY, Taking It Like a Woman

I

She was born in a dark house,
daughter of Eve, Adam's despair;

he grew to love her –
after all, wasn't she enchanting? –

and in return she snaked her way
through pink and blue.

Her mother galloped astride
her sewing-machine. It sang.

To older sisters she was a pram to push,
responsibility, another one the same,

but smaller. She was weaned
on dreams of someone...somewhere...else.

II

A six-year old summer shimmered
with static: glass absorbing,

glass reflecting, glass enclosing;
the TV's kaleidoscope seduced her.

(It was black and white at home.)
She was sitting on a man's knee,

quiet and cosy as an armchair.
He spreads her legs in a V.

Hot fingers trace rims of nylon knickers.
Then go in. It tickles.

She sinks into giggles,
the flesh of his thighs, wants

to open her legs wider, shut them
like scissors, both at the same time.

The man still watches the TV screen;
says it's cricket.

III

Every Saturday night she wore a different dress
and her father, blazer-spruce, held her hand,

led her into fluorescent halls.
She'd sip Coca-Cola through a paper straw

and pretend not to notice her Dad
winking at the ladies with eyes like witches',

babycham cherry lips, while her mother
sat at home, counting the sequins on *Come Dancing.*

She'd climb onto the stage to sing with the band –
songs about True Love and how sad it was.

Then she'd pick her way through puddles of applause,
and swaying men would peel back her fingers

and press half-crowns into her palm,
before going outside to beat each other up.

IV

If you stand in the middle of the rec
and spin, you feel on top of the whole wide world.

Your stomach somersaults:
as if you're dying and loving it.

You end up reefed in a knot on grass
and the sky winds round and round.

Boys cling like snot to the pavilion,
too shy, or scared, to ask for what they want.

They want you to go with them,
to the backwater, the metal hut, where,

inside, shadows echo and earth reeks –
a farmyard smell. The boys

want to be bulls, want to promise you
anything in the world, if you'll only

let them in yours.

V

The headmistress was one of the old school,
ink-black, bible-black, bat-black.

Her girls writhed like silver eels
down corridors of cabbage-water.

'No running.' 'No talking.' 'No
hair to be worn loose below the collar.'

'Skirts will not reach more than three inches
above the knee when in a kneeling position.'

'No one will mention politics or death or
sex.' 'We do not draw attention

to ourselves.' 'We are good girls,
polite girls.' 'The school colour is grey.'

She was one of the lucky ones:
she swam out of reach of the net.

VI

Down at the Boy's Club they let
girls in for the Friday night discotheque.

The wooden floor subsides in streams
of flashing lights. We dance in lines,

our shiny shoes shuffling to the Motown beat;
our new-grown hips tilt and swing, don't quite fit.

The boys ring the dark, smoking cigarettes,
looking casual; they only dance the slow ones.

24

We try to keep at bay their rodent chins
but soon melt into the wetness of a clumsy kiss.

No need for conversation – the noise
drowns it all. We fall in love with boys

who smell like our fathers, with their names,
unaware our mothers ever did the same.

VII

Sixteen singled him out: tall, dark
and beautiful – her rule-breaker, love-maker.

He sat at the wheel of an old red car, took
her to pubs where she learnt to smoke

and drink Bacardi with her Coke.
He brought her poems in ebony ink,

words crackling with desire – an ache
she also felt, and gave back,

rhyme by rhyme. He only had to look
at her and she'd crack

into a thousand pieces of fairy-tale luck.
They slept on beds of clover.

The little girl thought she was growing up.

VIII

She adjusts her smile like a woman,
so the creases of her sadness won't show.

('Charlie's dead' they say if a slither
of lace drags below a hem.)

He's not dead, nor she,
but her wounds scream. She wants to be

a nun, not a nurse. She packs
away the poems, the photos, in a box

under her bed. She sleeps like a virgin
who keeps serpents for pets. Hiss...

...Hiss. The woman adjusts her spectacles,
reads *The Bacchae, The Iliad* –

her cold fingers count the brief chorus
between her and the heroes.

IX

At the University, horn-rimmed tutors
tell her: 'Ideas are libidinal

cathexes, that is to say, acts of love.'
She doesn't believe them.

The words are brittle as dry sticks;
she sluices them down the river

of her tongue and seduces her own
'O's and fricatives. She is centuries old,

knows the slow odours of ocean
colours. She curls her body

into a 'C'; she swims like a fish,
to catch a fish. The hook

of her nail tears his mouth.
His blood washes them both clean.

X

'I tried death
                    but it was boring.
And I'm a coward
                    when it comes to death.

You saved me from black, and yellow,
the white terror of not knowing

where I ended and everyone else began.
You began.

Your golden hair bewitched me,
my Rumpelstiltskin. Will I ever know

your name? In the blur of wheels spinning,
glasses lifted and lowered,

something happened. Something important.
I ended; I began.

You ended; you began.
             We began.'

XI

She had a son – a scorpion
who stung her with palindromes

of white towelling, a mouth
that sucked, a tail that shat.

He grew, made room for more –
all sons, all men. Even the cats

were toms, prowling in the cruel night –
a wake of small brown morning corpses...

In her candle-rosy kitchen, she was the baker
of cakes, the producer of stews,

an apron armouring her milky breasts.
She stirred. She stirred.

She stopped watching the pot.
It boiled.

XII

Her father dies.
She feels his ghost brush her cheek.

She wakes from a dream full of men
to a world full of men,

and goes in search of more:
a woman looking in a mirror

to find out who she is.
She thinks the cracks are beautiful.

She must step on the cracks
and wait for the sky to fall.

The sky stays where it is.
She turns a perfect somersault,

stays on top.

XIII

'Imagine': she's looking back
down the long tunnel of years.

There's no light, whichever
end she stands. The tunnel's

lined with faces staring, voices
echoing, stairways that rise and fall.

All she can say is 'I am here'
and 'He...and he...and he is there.'

There are certain spells for
bidding, for binding, for blessing.

She'll weave them through the warp
of her dreams and suck her fingers

when the needle pricks.

North and South

Back in 1962 the world was
A foreign place I was just beginning
To feel at home in. I'd mouth and tongue sounds
My ears heard – Mam's clipped consonants, big sisters'
Sing-song vowels. And people understood.

Then one night was a dream of a red room
With wheels that kept me awake, stars spelling
South. South. South, where it never snowed and we
Would live in a nice new house and I would
Go to a nice new school.
                                    No one warned me.

Hamworthy Primary was full of kids
With straw between their teeth that made them sound
Like lazy cows. Where I came from the talk
Was quick as flocking birds. We laughed out loud –
No sneering behind hands, with rolling eyes.
Who's her? I cried inarticulate tears.

To survive, I had no choice but to try
To make my mouth echo back their fat *ain'ts*,
Become a chewing cow; or at least pretend.
I parroted their slow accents, even
Though the long feathers never really fit.
I plucked them out, the first chance I got;
But discovered I'd also lost, mid-flight,
My native accent I thought was bone.

In its place was this anonymous voice,
That sounds, to me, as if it belongs to
Someone else; feels two or three sizes too large.
The words and the spaces between the words
Ring with false echoes, false compass points.

My Red Letter

Someone had to be On It. Back turned,
she stood at the top of the summer garden
and called out letters, specifying steps –
pigeon or giant. You moved forward
a little or a lot, if the letter happened
to be a jewel in the necklace of your name.

O.K. Except I had no middle name,
fewer jewels. The others all had *Elizabeths*
or *Margarets* and coasted ahead
on their showy vowels and consonants.
I had to invent a *Cherry* or a *George*,
slipping them on like borrowed frocks.

And like second-hand dresses, they itched
or tickled; the clipped lawn under my toes,
drifts of small proud hybrid backs,
their perennial names. Me, annual,
but insistent, growing sure of something:
each season's petal fall; garnets; rubies.

Beginner's Luck

Like palm-sized counters in a child's game,
beneath the low lights the chips are stacked
in a haphazard rainbow city – mauve, orange, grey.
Her little tower is speckled yellow, marked
with crescent moons, a single star.

This is a nocturnal world, with new rules,
artificial-lit, where wild night creatures, pale-faced,
pink-eyed, vampires' kissing cousins, fall prey
to chance, the next stake sure as death and taxes.

Not-Bond-girl-beautiful, fat and bored
in polyester tat, the croupiers sweep the punters'
dreams from beds of green baize, blandly folding
crisp notes, deft as nursemaids.

But she catches the buzz like chicken-pox,
following the toss and spin of the silver ball,
clicking in and out of reds and blacks:
the fascination; the little flutter; a kid
again, in the Penny Arcade.

At the Black Jack table *Black Jack Pays
3 to 2, Insurance pays 2 to 1*. But not even
the attentive Oriental sipping lemon tea
from a glass is insured against the turn
of a card, her lucky birthday number.

Matching white for white this fresh hell's teeth,
she's taking greedy bites of a rotten apple,
juices fizzing on her tongue. *See you again!*
a starched dark bouncer calls. Cinderella
without a shirt, she smiles.

Razor

Their Midsummer ritual was not of fire:
white plastic razors,
hygienic, disposable.
They scalped him, head and neck;
from Viking warrior to Buddhist monk.

And now in bathroom intimacy,
watching him shave,
hearing the scrape of blade on bristle,
she remembers her father in front of the mirror,
craning his chin beneath a Christmas beard.

And her adolescent legs, seaside gold
and downy, shaved statue-smooth.
Once she held her father's razor
at too sharp an angle and a long slice of calf
dripped blood on the living-room carpet.

If she looked in the bed-sit mirror,
it would be like watching a play: one wrist,
then the other. But there wasn't a single blade
in the house – just glass.
She's skating over such sharp edges now.

Solstice Song

I want my mouth to make abstract nouns
that I can pluck from golden trees
like apples, cup their small globes
in one hand, bite, eat.

But by some sad magic they evaporate,
kisses blown in air, fantasies of skin;
a haunting tune in a minor key,
uncertain of the next note, rise or fall.

Unlike an abstract noun, the sun, they say,
is standing still; the best kind
of lover, vital, luminous, and always there,
even when you're chilled by moonlight.

Like a truth-teller at a wedding
no one can look in the eye, the sun
is standing still. Scrolls of cloud,
pure white, unfurl; cool the burning.

Even the sun melts into a brand
of abstraction I can't name, can't own;
only know the way it scorches my lips
with webs of abstract nouns, their shadows.

And so the sun at Solstice
mimes a spectacle of standing still,
whilst digging its own grave, singing
dirges that sting like bees, sweet thunder.

Turk's Cap Lilies in a Blue Vase

Their stout green stems
jungled with spears of leaves
draw attention to themselves,
boasting a jostling imbroglio
of yellow-rigged sultans.
Citrus skins flick back, flashing
a dumb-show of blood-orange teeth,
Scheherezade's cock, crowing.
Half-baked buds droop
like sleeping penises, green bananas.
They rise in a pulsing cloud of scent;
pepper, a cook's too-indulgent hand.
Or the smell-taste that comes together
of semen. It makes me want to bite.

> The vase is new; I can see
> my face in its smooth blue,
> an underwater creature
> preserved by salt, sheer glass.

No More Windows
(for Mike Barker, 1944-88)

The magnolia room bloomed with only eyes,
above sterile masks meant to protect you,
concealing loving conspiracies of lies.

And that uneasy sanctuary denies
the comfort of lips that can kiss and moue.
You soon grew tired of blank walls of muffled sighs.

It hurt. The pain inside climbed behind your eyes.
First, sight, then no more windows to feel through.
What clear words are there to say when a friend dies?

They buried you beneath wet sycamore skies.
Onto pale oak and polished brass, friends threw
flowers – roses, sweet william and ox-eyes.

After, in the damp village hall, everyone tries
not to drown in sadness, toasting you
with Irish tunes, whiskey, emerald goodbyes.

Your daughter looked at me with her anxious eyes,
brown and plaintive, like a dog's; yours were too.
And your brother's voice, with the same soulful rise.
The sky shoots black arrows of single magpies.

The Pain Business

1. *Apocryphal*

Somewhere there's a photo I've never seen
of my grandfather, valiant, thin

in woolly vest and baggy shorts, fists cocked
at Jimmy Wilde, flyweight champion, circa 1910.

My grandfather didn't win. The fight
and the photo were good enough for him,

my father, me. He hit and got hit
to fill out a pitman's wage, rising

from dark tunnels, a mole with restless paws,
coming up to scratch. He'd give my sisters

a penny each, big as their palms.
We never met.

I wouldn't even know him if I saw him
in black and white, hanging from a wall

of the Men Only bar in Blackett Street.

2. *Significant Other*

A ring that's square; canvas vast, clean
as a god's eye; three thick ropes, holding them in.

A couple of strangers, bodies shimmering
like cadillacs, fists flexed with half a pound

of cowhide, shotgun stares. Dream the way
their sweat smells – creased leather;

a week's work in each armpit: layered
with bathroom disguise, elbowed and punched.

Recall a child covering her face
with her hands at some curdling sight –

a beast with teeth, a tonguing snake – unable
to resist peeping through the cracks, not

wishing to miss what she didn't want to see.
She's here again, sitting at the ringside,

inching in some place she's not meant to be.

3. *Slinging Leather*

He hits the streets, a kid never much nimble
with words, dealing in punches and insults.

Some sharp white guy, steamrolling a cigar
between his teeth, teaches him how to box,

not fight – chess with muscles – dancing
on canvas, playing pat-a-cake, eating eggs,

steak. Better fed than a cotton-picking slave,
he looks tough, keeps his trap shut.

His super-hero's chest's mahogany,
polished so high you might see your face in it.

He want's to be the best, world champ;
will risk killing for it, being killed.

Knocked out in the gutter like an empty can
or crimsoning a bouquet of soft white towels –

he reckons the odds are even.

4. *Natural Selection*

A white carnation – *Dianthus*
caryophyllus – shares a black boxer's name,

the thin petals whorled
like a cauliflower ear.

Pain is a seed sown every season,
vital as bread, tobacco, booze;

its dangerous blooms – *Dementia*
pugilistica – commonplace as cabbage.

Everything in the garden's punch-drunk, reeling.
A rose might be a rose might be a rose

but considering the game, the rules,
is it true that everything is so dangerous,

nothing is really frightening?
Pour another drink. Listen

to your hand shaking.

5. *The Queensberry Rules*
Paris 1900

His cognac's running out. No one
left to stand another round. He sits

like a king whom gold has made a fool, mocked
by amber dregs. A man on one knee

is considered down. To hit's against the rules.
And hugging. When the bell rang to begin

and end the match, Bosie feinted the moves
Oscar desired; couldn't decide which

of his father's rules to follow.
The judges sat in his corner. He caught

him off his guard; fought below the belt.
Melmoth drains his glass; a prize-fighter

put out to grass, waiting for the long count.

6. *Southpaw*

Time was when rules were there to be broken;
now it's us who're tamed like horses, broken

in; mouths so full of tackle there's no room
for tongues, the articulate anarchy of kisses.

The danger's high as the stakes,
the fistful of cards close to the chest,

ducking under the left hook – impulse,
strategy, sweat. I watch my sons

limbering up to be men, can not put them through
their paces for an audience baying for blood.

They choke on tears if they think they've lost
and I wish my grandfather were there,

an impresario, mining pockets to press winking coins,
a white handkerchief into small steady hands

that can give or take a second skin.

Quayside
January 1991

The city's at war with itself,
brick buildings saluting the sky,
a battery of clapped-out guns.
In the tread of dusk, slick waters
bounce back hellish yellow lights,
fresh red neon, *Brett's Oils*.
Cousins of *Marie Celeste*, small-fry boats
wave frayed Union Jacks like apologies,
leftover festive tinsel and foil:
A Happy New Year and seven years' bad luck.
Even the boats give up the ghost;
a fleet of skips moored flat
on a rotten island isn't big enough
for half a sofa, an uprooted carpet
of muddy purple perennials,
what once was a cot.
You know the sort of stuff.
At the end of a stretch of warehouses
that look as if they know something
we don't, the Law Courts swank
like Noel Coward on gin-and-it,
slumming it, twinkling indomitable eyes.
All these are *New Developments*.
And so are a couple of urchin kids
playing laser games, ducking for cover
behind the *Esso-Esso-Esso* sign.
Convoys of cars chew up the road;
spit out someone else's Fourth of July.
And the bridge lift is full of piss,
laced with cosmetic chemicals.
In case of breakdown, stay calm.
Emergency services automatically alerted.
Out in the jackboot dark, at the kerbside
a streetlight illuminates a painted circle
containing the legend END.
This is a true story. Stay calm.

Under Byker Bridge

The man who's fond of maroon
wears turquoise, acrylic,
borrowed ochre.

An impromptu holiday,
quaffing lurid vodka, lime
and ice, tales of infidelity.

Forget rectangles,
blue, white, inevitable brown:
stroke the velvet of alcohol,

the Rothko on his wall,
dark shadows across the Thames,
the Tyne, glass reflecting

too much light: maroon
of blood and bull-hide,
drop by soothing drop.

Red-slaked, his secret
appetite's for black and white,
the poise of a kingfisher, zen.

Ladies

Betty Peggy Amelia Grace
Friends Always –
a wayward kiss punctuates
the message on the once-white wall.
The cursive script's felt-pen fresh,
an elderly school-certificate hand.
But was it Betty who brandished
her bingo pen? Maybe Peggy,
caught by the urge, autographed
her souvenir of a fine day out.
Or Amelia, tucking in her thermals,
thought *Well, what the hell?* Perhaps
it was the diffident Grace,
after a life-time of coming last,
who finally struck out to be the first
graffiti artist drawing a widow's pension.
Betty, Peggy, Amelia or Grace –
their billet-doux's a shock.
Unlike the ubiquitous brazen *cunt*
splashed on cracked ceramic.

Interflora

Your Californian poppies look like a million dollars,
blooming from their green envelope regardless –

Surcharge to Pay; With Love: a bouquet
of contradictions. Streaked cream, scarlet, jaffa,

lilac-pink, spreading their Kodachrome silks,
haute-couture tassels trimming each cupped centre.

This is Georgia O'Keeffe getting mellow,
singing a jazzy palette. For me. From you.

I should be with you tonight, drinking fine wine
we can't afford. I should be with you tonight,

playing the range of your colours, unpeeling your silks.
Sweetheart, the only word is gay, this blossoming.

We're simple girls, but damned bright, going West, after
intemperate dreams of skins like silk, glamour.

Dutch Interior

Let's say this light-filled space is the Netherlands
and I am one of that loose knot
of people unravelling themselves, making
straight for the edge. I am
one of those people, but there are two of us.

There's an old farmhouse with a barn
full of left luggage. I'm climbing over
the sheer domestic mess of it
when one of us disappears. My foot balancing
on a yellow cup, I think I may well fall.

The next thing, I'm weaving through
simple rooms, along corridors, looking for
the one that got away; loss hovering
beneath low ceilings like the smell
of coffee when it's not there.

I tell everyone I'm a visitor, lying
in a foreign language. It only makes it worse
when they smile and offer me tea.
The pragmatic light waves its white flag.
More than that, I really can't say.

Bluebell and Father Are Different Words

Bluebell and *father* are different words,
meaning different things, with different
sounds. I know this from before.
Before that May's silent hyphen punctured
both, hissing dusty echoes in mauve

air. Driving home from his grave, my mother
sat in the back; his usual place next to me
carved in the choked air. *Thunder*
means weather, black, red and silver:
the sudden colours of the crash, falling

from a dumb sky; May, unlucky, in the air.
My mother like a backstage puppet,
her eyelids jammed. On her lap, the dog
barking, barking. Then, a muted silence.
No sense or sounds for sharing spill

from shapes my mouth makes. Just thin
night noises, thin air. I've lost something
so important I can't remember what it is.
All I find is no one saying the words
Not your fault. Pebbles in my throat,

pockets of infested air, I swallow them
like pills; know them well as old enemies.
Air's not what it seems, faking its cool *empty*,
its *invisible*; dreams smothered
with bluebells, wreaths of fresh air.

Samantha

It's funny seeing your own face looking
back at you from the newspaper, not smiling
and neat like the photos we have taken

at school. I've been on telly too. Three times.
Thought I'd be scared but they were dead nice;
gave me a paper cup of orange juice.

I've told the story of the hospital, the foster home, so many
times I dream it every night. I don't cry
any more. What I feel most is angry.

They wouldn't let me go home. That's all
I wanted. Not that silly stupid doll
with nothing on the social worker called

Sam and told me I should
point to all the places where he'd touched
me. When I said it wasn't true they wouldn't

believe me. My Dad says it's wrong to lie.
But even though I tried
to convince them, they didn't listen. So I

said yes in the end; lied. Thought they'd let me home.
She gave me some paper to write the person's name
on. I only wanted to be with him, and Mam

again; back here in my own room, my bed
with the pink quilt. Downstairs, Mam and Dad,
their voices humming through the floorboards.

It worked for a girl I saw on the telly
once. Wonder if *she* lied. She looked a bit like me,
eyes all pinched up, scared of what they'd see.

Sea Nymph

My home was always ocean, liquid blue
thinned to spirit, salt. My days and nights
were swimming; star-mirrors fished from sand,
dead men's eyes. I breathed dreams of pure azure.

Until the shadow of a god darkened
my sea, a three-pronged rod held high, aiming.
His sea-hunger fleshed into an earth-horse,
lunging after my waves, snorting thunder.

I was caught in his fat white teeth, kissed
by bone, swallowed like wine at a wedding.
He dived into me, deep and hard, staining
coral branches the colour of my blood.

Then ocean was no home, no clear freedom.
I've grown roots now to hold me down, feed me;
and my soft waist has thickened to bark.
My tears grow green, rust, fall; dry linden leaves.

Mary Josephine Travers Speaks, 1870

Ask any honest soul in Dublin, he's filth,
black as nail dirt, from scratching hisself.

Sure, you've heard the tale of Lady Spencer,
the Viceroy's wife, who went to dinner:

she spotted his fat grimy thumb dip
in the tureen, and refused to eat any soup.

But when I was poorly with my eyes,
who else could I go to but Sir William Wilde,

Surgeon Oculist in Ordinary to the Queen?
I was only a young girl then, green

as shamrock, innocent as a lamb. I didn't suspect
a thing when he took out his chequered

handkerchief, padded it round my nose.
But I felt so drowsy. I dozed

like a farmer after too much poteen.
Not so far gone though not to feel

his fumbling at my skirts, nor to see Sir
William Wilde grinning like a satyr.

Bejasus, my eyes weren't that bad.
I'm a strapping girl, but for my eyes; pushed him off, I did;

took him to Court. Criminal Assault
they called it. He said it was just alleged.

Sued me for libel. Sure and guess who won?
I got nothing but an English farthing –

damages. But it was his good name was damaged,
more than a golden guinea. He never recovered.

Mind, I suffered too. A scandal puts
men off, and my pebble spectacles.

Susan Martin, Painter's Wife

Forty-five ruby-red years we were married,
years as stormy as those extravagant paintings
he seemed to adore more than me.

I remember long hours reading aloud,
as he messed with his palettes and brushes,
the lurid fumes of oils fisting my lungs.

The focus of his eyes set his visions on fire,
as sunlight through glass. He'd fan the crimson
flames. I'd melt; continue reading.

Soon I was too busy for *Paradise Lost*:
six children to rear, three to bury;
and money stretched as tight as canvas.

A pity his purse never matched his popularity.
I shiver at the expense of his plans for London
that came to nothing. So practical, black and white.

Now he's dead, there's little left. All our gifts
from kings and lords and princes sold at auction.
Just some chaotic pictures, a fading name.

And me, a rheumatic old woman,
telling the tale of someone else's life,
waiting for a death to call her own.

Edward Hopper's *Hotel Room* (1931)

What the hell am I doing here,
a cheap hotel room in Baltimore?

The crowded streetcar reeked of greasy
done-in flesh. I looked so classy

in my new cloche and heels, it ruined
the effect. They pinch my feet. It's good

to get them off. I've read this letter
too many times already. The elevator

was out of order. I walked up three flights,
counting each stair. Room twenty-five.

It's passably clean but cramped,
with a monstrous chair, old-fashioned, emerald,

and leftover layers of other people's affairs.
What did I expect? Straight after work, he says,

he'll call by. A whole night and breakfast
together before he drives on up to the Adirondacks

to join his wife and kids. He's signed it just
with his initial, a thin spidery kiss.

I told Mom and Dad their little girl's
staying over at Doreen and Earl's

place; they're covering for me. I wanted
this. When we're apart I feel so odd,

incomplete. But that's how it is right now. Maybe
someday he'll leave his kids, and her, for me.

I saw this movie at the Ritz the other day...
Aw, sitting here, I'm getting nervous, the way

I am waiting to see my dentist. We've never
gone all the way before. All that yellow,

like eggs, sunny-side up, turns my stomach,
the puce counterpane. Hope he'll crack

some bourbon. It's ten after six. Guess
I ought to dress. Just so he can take it off again.

Jesus, I'm scared. What am I doing here?
It wasn't like this in the movie.

The Song of Solomon's Wife

O I was stiff as bitter aloes, green
as sharp cypresses in sweet Lebanon.
And how I drowned in his shower of kisses,
his promises, my unripe olive flesh
fizzing with fresh musk, the shock of desire,
melting like wax round a wick all on fire.
I should have known all those slick lines about
perfect white teeth were so much sheep-rot.
O daughters of Jerusalem, never
believe any man who compares your breasts
to a cluster of dates or twin gazelles.
You'll feel the prick of his tines. When he tells
you your lips are scarlet ribbons, he means
he has a fancy for playing with chains
and leather. *Your mouth breathes the lush bouquet
of vineyards* translates as he could murder
a jug or two of strong wine. Don't listen
to anything he says except to plan
your excuses. If in doubt, fly the red
flag: seeming suitably sanguine, allude,
shyly, but regularly to blood – old
as the hills of Gilead, never known
to fail. Trust me, O women of Zion,
for I know. With pomegranates and palms,
I've sown my shady garden, my mirror
of pleasure. Come close and let me whisper.
Ah, I see from the roses in your cheeks
you share the open bloom of my secret.
Good. Another path is more dangerous.
But there's safety for deer hunted in pairs.
Climb down from your cold white marbled towers,
fill your laps with buds of country flowers.
Pluck a new lover to fuck like a fox
in the forest, someone whose right hand knows
what her left is doing, who's ripe enough
for her milk not to have turned sour. Take heart
from the song of a wife skilled in the art
of singing with stags on the mountains where spices grow.

Call Me Kitten

Even the screws call me *kitten*.
Runs off the tongue better
than the number you wouldn't call a dog.
Home says its to do with how I'd curl up
in cupboards when I were young.
                              Priest came
and wanted to know why
I've got a tattoo says *I hate people*.
You show me the cats in churches.
Doesn't even know what's a cat
and what's a lion. It's not worth
wasting your breath.
                    No cats
in this place either. So I draw them.
Governor's into Art Therapy
so I get more paper than a public bog.
As long as I keep my arse clean,
they're happy. And as long
as I'm drawing cats,
                    I'm away.
Bloke I share with says
they give him the heeby-jeebies –
I tell you, they're beauties – all slinking
after him with their narrow eyes.
Lights out and they still do it.
Just goes to show.
                  I stroke
the cats prowling my dreams. Wake up
to stone walls and my cats' mouths,
they're all red, wet
with blood. Old yellow-belly's nothing
but bones under his mangy blanket.
The barred sun burns a hole
in my brain. Fresh air,
clean as a cat's mouth,
                        yawning.

Stateless

Tavarisch is a dirty word. Blue-pencilled
like an official secret. The built-in obsolescence
of perestroika, Leningrad, Space Station Mir.
My mother was so proud. Now Cosmonaut Krikalev
is just a repairman, Robinson Crusoe in overalls,
a hero for a country that doesn't exist.

When I was afraid of the dark, my mother
told me I could switch it on, like light.
And she'd show me the stars, families
of silver bears. Now I can't switch it off.
So many different shades of black,
clouds of stars and sewage. The only
lovely thing is earth, tantalising,
forbidden as a black-market apple.

First, the floating frogs kept us busy,
research. Then the quail chicks started
dying and everything went wrong like a joke
won't survive re-telling. I'm still
waiting for the punch-line: choke
on the glutinous food, reconstituted air.
Nothing like home. My family on TV
at the weekends: coloured postcards
I can't keep. I switch off the machine,
stare at its dark. Get back to my exercises.

I don't know if there'll be a party
when I come home: dancing, scarlet
in the streets, my name in the stars, medals
forged from melted missiles. Anything
would be better than what I don't know
already, everything I know about dark.

1492 and Counting

Sorry, we have this many bananas.
How many kids. My wife and me. Bigfoot,
our pet iguana, he fend for himself.
Plenty insect. Last week we lucky
with frog. But now not so many,
not so many trees. Sometimes I look
at the children. No meat. I say
José, you turning into a monster?
A very little one.

But our heads up in clouds, big space
between trees. We all runts, house
no more than a pig pen. They say
there are bins in cities overflow
with food nobody need. When kids bigger,
I tell them go see if it true, maybe
get a decent meal.

Every night there's always how many.
I say *the birds bring you home*
through the forest? It's not they follow
smell of cooking. We go to bed early.
To rest the air in our stomach.
Everyone seeing pictures
of steaming pots of rice and beans;
trees grow, strong, tall,
like healthy children.

Do Not Speak to the Ansafone
(with apologies to Ted Hughes)

That fallen angel yawns a thudding hum

Before the lost words crackle
The transparent apology

Satan invented the ansafone it was built in the pit of Satan
Do not hobnob with the ansafone
It wraps its pawns in broken promises
Speaks in many tongues   silver   forked

Keep mute when you hear the malevolent snore of the ansafone

Do not think you deserve an answer you'll get an ansafone
Do not think the word is flesh it is an ansafone
Do not think your diary is yours it is at the mercy of an ansafone
Do not think your ear is sound it is polluted by the ansafone
Do not think you have the power to act in the passive face of the
         ansafone
Do not think time is time it is the monotonous click of the ansafone
The infernal tyranny of the ansafone

O ansafone evaporate
You are an arrogant phantom
Go and roar in some other storm
Do not wink your rodent eye at me
Do not gnaw at my simple needs

You telekinetic hack
Why must you play the honest juggler?
How do you choose your stooges?

Out your words ooze
like rancid honey   a castrated drone

A seductive familiarity couches your monologues
And though your audience is never guaranteed
When a victim presents a brace of simple sentences
You suck them through your promiscuous lips and spit them out

56

Or ignore them
Stranding your scapegoat
Exposed in a cyclone of silence

The playful hiss and innocent whistle
Of your tone are intended to mislead
You're invisible   anarchistic
Impossible to plead with
You negotiate with no one

Do not speak to the vacuum of the ansafone
A foul-breathed harpy will gibber out of the ansafone
A demon will steal your soul and give it to the ansafone

Do not speak to the ansafone

On First Looking into Raymond Chandler

Of course I always knew who you were. I
grew up with Humphrey Bogart, Hollywood.
I used to think everyone talked that good.
Then, browsing a second-hand bookstall, I
saw this faded green and cream Penguin. Five
pence, the man said. For Church funds. I handed
it over, took you home to read in bed.
Some nightcap. The only place I went was wide-
awake, dreaming of California,
where the high-life's pretty low and the heat
shimmers like your prose. I could feel it all,
cool as anything, on the rocks, or neat.
Now your hero's mine too, and you can call
anytime and find me right on your beat.

Dead Fish Don't Tell Tales

Hitching rides a girl's
always taking a chance,
but listen to this –
Dashiell Hammett, a dead fish
and me in an old saloon car
on Halloween –
that's more than something.

The man with the tender eyes
just got himself shot
on page four; what did I want
with a dead fish?

The car's exhaust lacked any sense
of occasion and from where I sat
it reeked of smoke. I sniffed,
failing to detect the slightest
whiff of fresh river.

The fish lay inert next to me
on the back seat, jutting
its dead head out of a plastic bag
that called itself *Safeway*.
So what's new?

There was some uneasy eye contact.
The fish's thin lips
drew themselves wide
in a dumb angry yell.

I felt so sorry for that fish.
We practically had a relationship.
Some guy's supper,
while I was heading home
for a plate of pumpkin pie,

tales of dead things
round the fire.

Sheep, Hens

My first bite of morning: field
scumbled with light, sheep, hens.
Sheep ragged, inert as hay-bales,
shingled with snow, white
on dirty white; their rude
poker-faced stares require no
introduction before follow-my-leader
they slip their moorings, roll
adenoidal *r*s at a flash-
forward breakfast of turnips, nuts.
In my briefcase there's only paper, books.
Hens dance on snow-shoe feet
spurred on by the gigolo cock.
In loose formation they suck crystal
through dipping beaks, eyes
on horizons they'll never reach.
I have an appointment at 10.15.

Later, in the carpet and chrome
of the coffee-house, mud clinging
to my boots, I observe snow
melt through glass; impossible
to listen to the low trickle
inside my head for the echoing din,
baas, clucks.

Runaway

It was dark when we came home,
door still jammed as if she'd shut it
behind her, covered her tracks.
A cold black doglessness.

It's hard to say what I missed most:
waggish ears; her casual furstyle;
polished eyes under politician's brows;
her Guinness jig; tabor of her tail;
or that bark I could pick out
a bone's throw from Battersea Dog's Home.

But nothing. Nothing but a flat tangle
of straw, a half-eaten dish of Poacher's.
We spent all evening not talking about dogs,
seeming to listen to the jazz on Radio 3,
tuned in to the wind growling at the curtains.

Midnight kept us awake
till a small canine voice called
to us to open the door, like a teenage son
who'd forgotten his key. She was pure skulk
until she remembered she was our best friend.
And that was what her tongue was for.

Imaginary Landscape with Real Horse

Imagine the blur of day turning into grey
evening, dusk lowering its soft pad on the land,

still river – a deep wash of essential blue, grey,
submerged jade. Then this shock of white, static

marble. Each step nearer pulses its own echo
of white – dream; mirror; flesh. Horse. She walks

across the floating paddock, rolling her fetlocks.
The great black globe of her eye hurls itself

right to the heart of me. And all I'm saying
is *Horse!* stroking her boned cheek, her bold trust.

I want to climb the fence, and her; ride
bareback over the hills, all one with laughing,

this crisp close night, its intimate moon
and few fresh stars; a female centaur shot from

the arrow of earth on the verge of spring.
This snorting creature takes my breath away.

And gives it back: our aspirations,
airy wildness mingling.

The Key to the Kingdom

As if to a small child you explain the rules:
that I must travel through the kingdom
in search of the Golden Key lying hidden
amidst other treasures in bleak castles,
wierd buildings. It won't be an easy journey
as fantastic hazards, mythical monsters
will bar my path. You make the Bone Pit,
Rat Trap and Whirlpool sound like our front garden.
As real as that. And I'd swear you'd visited
the Temple of Martyrs, the Banshee Towers
before. Without even letting me know.
I'm at sea, keep to the stepping stones.
Though nowhere looks safe in my kitchen right now:
all those grisly creatures – Mutant Scorpion,
Dreaded Druid, Alien Stalker, Corpse Lord –
all rising to the surface like bubbles
in Beelzebub's stew, demanding
I brandish my grappling hook or axe
or other useful tool I happen to have
about my fearless well-prepared person.
At the far side of the table there's a stack
called *Deep Magic.* Whatever it is,
I fancy some of it, a magic carpet
or invisible cloak to spirit myself
away. I seem to be catching the thread
of this, this fantasy virus but can't
summon up enough heroic flair
to attempt to *win.* I sit back, off my guard,
losing disgracefully (*like a girl* – worse
than any monster), simply amazed
at your excited fidgeting, your faces
glowing from the ordeal, your beady eyes.
I wonder if either of you finds
the Key to the Kingdom you'd consider
sharing. A favour for your mother.
Or else you catch your own Wild Boar for supper.

Elementary
(for Rufus)

I ask my son what he knows of earth,
of properties of metal,
the rings in the heart of wood,
what shapes he can trace in air,
how deep is the blue of water;
remind him to take care with fire.

He has a dangerous fondness for fire,
my son, learning the lessons of earth;
knows magnets are science, metal,
observes their attraction through water.
He's aware that a kite, and he, needs air,
the paper he'd miss so much is wood.

We scramble hand in hand through the wood
near our house, feeling the damp earth
spring under our feet, the lapping of water
in the silence. The cold air
makes him cough so we go home to the fire,
welcomed by kettle's singing metal.

His toys are plastic; mine were metal,
with sharp corners. They rusted in water.
Now the fashion's back for wood,
carved and painted trains, trucks and fire-
engines. Things have changed. This earth
I thought I knew, and love, is mutable as air.

My son was four the year the air
blew from the east, poisoned by fire,
a fire kindled with no wood.
The smell of my sweat was metal.
We couldn't trust rain, milk or earth,
were afraid to drink the water.

He loves to play in water,
and I to watch him, in the tenuous air
of summers. I lean against knotted wood,
by the river glinting metal.
As certain as flames in fire
we're held in the breath of earth.

I pray to the gods of air, goddesses of wood
and water, that he'll be saved from fire,
and save, like precious metal, all he knows of earth.

Falling

Blinded by black dimensions of dreams,
an unfamiliar room, waxing moon falling,
lost, towards a net of invisible stars,

I dance down the inner edges of dark.
The low wide window's a door falling
onto blurred horizons of sky, crags, moor.

Seeing by the light feel of my fingers,
unable to catch the connection falling
through my grasp – window, body, danger –

I launch myself from the smooth plank
of the sill; a pair of sycamore wings falling,
like breath, out of season to earth.

This is what air feels like and how
it doesn't carry you if you're falling
through it – quick and cool and light as nothing.

Then solid earth ups and plants itself between me
and ether: dew-damp soil, my hair falling
like uprooted weeds over the stone path,

and the narcotic scent of crushed fennel
lacing the air, my prone naked body falling
awake to sounds of panic, flash of torches.

I'm stuck, flat as turf, and laughing;
but no words for this dream of falling
I can't switch off, yellow light stinging my eyes.

Snow Crazy

We're living in a time before colour
was invented; even before thought clawed
its way through stone and spread its spoor. We are
white people breathing ice in a white world.
Laughing, in virgin rows, flat on our backs,
we're making a snowy host of angels
to ward off the white demons falling thick
from the place that once was celestial.
This winter is innocence, paradise:
you can rely on everything being
white. Even the blacks and greys are all white.
And, mere shadows, we trail our own demons.
Here, hoof and wing are the same thing: both white,
both hell-bent on setting the white alight.

New York Spring

He had the nerve to say *Let's be grown-up about this.*
Like hell. And him acting like a kid who wants jello
with his Häagen-Dazs. Let him eat grown-up pussy.
With claws. I left as sharp as my little beauties.
All that stylish white we worked our asses off for
didn't look so clean after he told me what he told me
was all. Stupid, trying to deny a crop of blonde hairs
marbling the sheets when we're both shades of New England brown.
His downfall: never learning to use the washing-machine.

When a mutual friend let slip they'd gone away for a time,
I didn't even need to think; still kept the key
to the loft on my fob. Let myself in like a regular burglar,
come to claim something I couldn't take home in a bag
marked swag; but just as desirable. And it was as if I'd grown-up,
died a little and nothing I touched would ever be the same.
I exchanged greetings with the washing-machine,
borrowed its black snake of a hose and soaked the whole place
in high-pressure tears. All the things we'd bought together

and loved, I purified with water, an act of defiant surrender.
Good and wet, I sprinkled it thick with seeds
from the wholefood store, mustard and cress, 100% organic.
Millions of little dots, beige and ochre, an experiment
after Lichtenstein. Then I turned the heating on high,
shut the door up tight. The saddest thing is, I can only imagine
their faces when they opened the door, expecting
soothing sterile white, to find a ripening anarchy of green,
their very own pastoral symphony, its pungent smell addling the air:

my parting gift, a blessing grown despite neglect,
just a little something they'd never forget,
the colour of an old friend's eyes.

The White Crest on the Ninth Wave

Fireweed

The surprise of you is a purple rocket,
a green spiral stairway spinning its inevitable

up, down. I tell the eccentric amethysts
of your pedigree – Blood Vine, Blooming Sally,

Rose-bay Willowherb. You disdain to answer
to any but looking, uncommon sense, trawling

your heliotrope net. And now the slack year
folding into dark, your chameleon colours:

abandoned auburn cottons; proud
body-long stem crowned with smoke-ring curls

silking the damps. No perfume but the rain,
mead behind your ears, your spitting flames.

You've put the bees to bed. Death by fire
was never this gentle, this full of growing.

Nothing will be the same again. And *always,*
always your grande dame deshabillée voice

is husking, your phoenix eyes.

Touch and Go

Waiting is floating in a dense pool of salty air,
dreaming wisps of gravity, its stirring bugle hook.

As usual it lets you down: you're still there;
the air's still there. Steaming. And still no sign

of the cavalry. Horizontal, you're buoyant
as a mermaid, faking it, singing airs

to philistine fishes. The ocean's a mirror,
its hot red eye a net of bubbles, getting to you

like wine. You've lost your silver comb. Your hair
is a mess. Do you even care?

This is the amnesia of driftwood, a traveller
with ribs, no camera, too many creases

full of too much grit. If this is waiting,
give me flowers, Japanese, like chrysanthemums.

I'll tuck one inside my thigh. Call it dancing.
I'm in my element, a serpent's tooth.

The only antidote, whisky, a single flower.

Transit

The city has fallen, dragging you with it. Then,
such stillness. White sky. A single blue bird.

You must learn again how to conjugate
the verb *to be*; part its crimson, its curled

lips, the born-again business of kisses.
You're centre-stage, blissfully corpsing;

adrenalin's little death: the wrong sex
for metaphysics and swords. But the cap fits;

its feather nodding indigo dialectic.
Welcome to the cusp of change –

the electric chair in the corner
of a thousand sitting-rooms; the axis

of loss; a memo of bones.
Think of two words before you succumb:

blue bird. The next thought goes soaring,
and you are who you're meant to be.

Scry it flying. Plant snowdrops.

Confidence

Two empty tea cups, and we're still sitting.
Your silver spoon taps in morse: *Explain*.

Explain. My hands spin hoops and crescents,
shadows. They catch my meaning

like a waterfall doesn't. I'm in deep water;
a woman giving birth to herself.

Your eyes two black mirrors; the cave
of your mouth asking and asking.

I avoid words like *answer*, *future*;
leave a turquoise fragrance in the air

for you to take to the place people call home,
curtains drawn to keep out the moon.

And a storm of glass bubbles exploding
in your pores, your shining eyes, dark

and new. One day at a time, nights
in between: the seven sisters in the south-east

stirring their silver spoon; concentric circles.

At Seventeen

I am nearly twice her age – a girl
with braided hair framing squirrel eyes,

who lives in a dusty room inside her head;
goes out at nights, a parrot on parole.

She wears Liberty gloves; is writing
her own Bildungsroman, her emerald manifesto,

polishing the mote of her eye. She is a perfect
zoo, an endangered species.

Now she considers me, red and purple,
a bruised wound. I don't play by her rules.

Her question's an echo – concerned mother,
abused child: *why did it take me so long*

to come home? I give her the measure
of linen I've been stitching and unravelling,

stitching and unravelling; a calendar
of owls and acorns, all colours.

And we let down our chestnut hair.

On Ice

Treading frozen water, a silver wheel,
icicle spokes; two steps forward, one step back;

Jack Frost's teeth nipping my late buds:
the very idea of unfurling turned to ice;

hypnotic logic's death by sterilisation, shrouded
in off-the-peg inertia. The magic skates

are all sold out; frostbite scored white
behind the eyes. Ice, like this, is rigor,

a mirror which cracks from too much looking
into an iceberg rictus, a drowned smile;

cuts like glass, a red stain blooming
like a Rorschach blot, rimed petals of braille.

I'm playing Ophelia On Ice, a black pantomime
of choking weeds, a lost brother, northern cold.

Waking to winter's heavy-booted consonants
from a dream of thaw, I'm taunted by lilting vowels

of a forgotten song, water on the run.

Parabola

Someone will always cast the first stone. It falls
at my feet with a sound like *sin*.

It's impossible to take another step without a foothold
I didn't invent myself, Heath Robinson

on acid. The spell I thought was steel
is broken like ice too thin to skate on.

And the water is so bone-cold fresh
it splinters my eyes with tears that warm me

curiously, spin prism visions of illusions
I was in too much of a hurry to bless and bury

in their appropriate tarnished silvers. I must unpick
a shroud or two, continue darning. Dog-ends

of ice bite my fingers, burn my madonna hands
into a dream of black-winged birds migrating in fear,

black night's freedom. Even then the moon's at my back,
battering me with its sibilant beams,

like tears, like stone.

After the Fall

The sun's too bright for November, playing
with marked cards. Everything she sees casts shadows.

She's forgotten the knotted handkerchief
of her name; thinks it's forbidden, a four-letter word.

In her pocket instead there's a snake shedding the shadow
of its skin, paper-thin; and she's walking on webs.

Ignorance is bliss but knowledge is power.
Weighing them in the balance, she finds herself wanting.

And wanting. Wanting more than black and white,
more than anyone else can give. Here is the fulcrum:

the necessity of definition. Or notes towards...
Patience is a virtue. Virtue is a grace.

Grace is a girl with a dirty face.
She catches the snake winking its wise eye,

more skins tucked, like aces, up its sequinned sleeve.
Whatever her name is, it's not *easy*.

She'll be shady: survive.

Lunaria

Now I've folded myself in owl-moth quiet,
lit up the corners with scarlet spirals

of wax burning holes in the wainscot like mice.
This is some nights; a sort of peace: peeling

back thickened buff skins of honesty to free
the moon-silk discs beneath, raw mirrors

shedding light and dark. I let the seeds fall
on yesterday's news, small matte-black eyes,

the opposite of stars. I scatter them
and their dusty pods on the rotting fertile compost.

The vase of tangled dots is a grandmother's party frock
by candlelight, a ceiling tree, pearly skeletons

of flowers for over winter in a cold house,
with candles. No guidance from my reference books

for *Honesty*. But still the irresistible alchemy
of fire – an inch-long flame singeing white silk

by proxy; what was, and will be, purple.

The Bookbomb

It had been a perfectly ordinary day
up to that point: picking five hundred narcissi
(*pseudopoeticus*) from the front lawn, frilling
the house like a wedding dress, jonquils, innocence;
sex at the tea-table, blondes and brunettes – a saint
in a leopard-skin coat kicked a brass gong as soon
as anything began to get interesting.
Then, taking the lion and the cobra out
for a stroll before curried dugong for dinner,
poppa-poppa-poppadoms. So there I was,
a post-prandial dip in a book of poems
by an Irish poet I'd met in a bar once.
All perfectly ordinary. Like all the best
pleasures, vices. I take it you're still with me?
I've just finished the one about driving at night
in the desert when a piece of lined paper falls
into my fingers, apparently blank until
I unfold it: in pencil, the words *a bomb*
that explodes when you touch it. I don't know about
you, but I live a simple sort of life. Some things
you just can't help noticing. For example,
explosive devices. In the vernacular,
bombs. The next poem chased a painted skater.
I couldn't make any sense of it – the note, I mean –
the poem was consummately balanced. No, that
message, that *billet-doux*, that handwriting I failed
to recognise. Come to think of it, it wasn't
unlike the artistic scrawl of the Irish bard
when he showed me his poetic licence in the depths
of the Black Kesh. Or was I reading too much
between the lines? Hell, you can go on asking
questions *ad nauseam*. Stay patient and it all
falls into place; even chaos will assemble
its own order. And I've already stated
my position on the paranormal. The way
I see it, everything is more or less – read my lips –
perfectly ordinary. Reality is
something you invent, like a book; the cliché being,

truth is stranger than fiction. But poetry –
are you listening out there? – but poetry
positively explodes like a bomb when you touch it.
I infer from your silence that you agree.

The Insomniac

says *fuck* to the dark. She swears
the dark's listening but it's dumb

as a shut door. No manners. The silence
makes fists in her ears, knuckle-bone deaf.

She's awake and aching for oblivion,
the sleep of a virgin, the dreams of a whore.

So tired, so desperately tired, she'd kill
for a little white pill to still this pulsing,

a tourniquet for her heart. She's pumping out heat
like a radiator in a library, Centigrade, Fahrenheit.

She's re-running all the movies she's ever seen
in one showing. She's writing scripts for *Coming Soon.*

The birds outside her window start racketing;
sound so fucking happy to be awake.

She concedes the victory of light
and spends the day looking like a hostage,

unable to match the wide-eyed Walden stare
of six gorgeous fawns interrupted grazing

a clearing. She feels like the worst sort
of animal, those you don't read about in books,

those you don't count to get to sleep.

Lough

I am everyone's mother, eyes in the back
of my head. What I don't see isn't worth

seeing. I have a fresh colour for every day
of the week, all weathers; a clean frock,

new jewels. Simply the centre of attention,
my age is a secret I'm not sharing. I keep

everyone guessing. They haven't enough words
for my greys. They stare, they row, they fish;

they convince themselves they know me. But no one
can walk on my water. Those who tried

I swallowed; their bones feed my bed. At night
I dance with the moon; make a little light

love. Never sleeping, my dreams are still
water. If I were to tell you everything…

but I brook no bridges. Whisper in my ear
all you like, *lough, lough, lough.*

Hedge Laundry

The sun strokes the thin skin of the sky,
opaque and absent-mindedly warm;
spills on the greening flat-topped hedge
that's the next-door cottage's washing line,
a floral dance of towels and shirts and vests,
tip-to-tip hooked on spikes of poking branches;
fills their flattened spaces, their open-weave
with summer air, bleaching them clean and dry,
lightening the burden of another wearing.
Their phantom forms – uncrumpled by days
spent pounding tarmac, spines beaten into iron,
nights bending backwards, playing chameleon –
stretched back to the shape of perfection,
a remembered Eden where everything is in touch,
in its element, no flaws, or loose ends,
and all linen is clean; everything fitting
a mathematical formula that's death
to a thousand pencils. The full open air's a mirage
of stillness, cloaking the imperceptible bleaching
of threads, the way colour evaporates,
how a ladybird, creeping along the chequered
carriageway of a cotton collar, lays the trail
of a tickle, a freshness to breathe in:
the clean shirt sweeping new, as near
as you'll get to fresh skin, an improved model;
another chance to sample the theories,
wear your clean linen as good as new,
a new thing under the sun stroking your skin.